Pelham Pictorial Sports Instruction Series

Rachael Heyhoe Flint
WOMEN'S HOCKEY

Photographs by Gordon Jones

Pelham Books

Also in the Pelham Pictorial Sports Instruction Series

Bob Wilson : Soccer
John Dawes : Rugby
Chester Barnes : Table Tennis
Barry Richards : Cricket
Richard Hawkey : Squash Rackets
Henry Cooper : Boxing

In preparation

Ken Adwick : Golf
Paul and Sue Whetnall : Badminton
Jack Karnehm : Understanding Billiards
and Snooker

First published in Great Britain by
PELHAM BOOKS LTD
52 Bedford Square
London WC1B 3EF
1976

ISBN 0 7207 0806 0

Printed in Great Britain by
Fletcher & Son Ltd, Norwich

Contents

Foreword

Women's Hockey is an instructional book which will be of great value to those wishing to learn to play Hockey and in need of expert guidance.

Mrs Rachael Heyhoe Flint is an all-round sportswoman, a first-class performer in many games and is one of the select band of women who have represented their country in two sports — in this case Hockey, where she has played as Goalkeeper for England ; and Cricket, where she is the current Captain of the England Women's Cricket XI. An experienced coach with knowledge of all aspects of the game, her sound advice on the techniques and method of play is enhanced by the excellent action photographs which illustrate the text.

Throughout its existence, the All England Women's Hockey Association has given priority in its activities to the coaching of the game, arranging courses for all grades of players as well as producing instructional films and coaching manuals, to which this book is a welcome addition.

I confidently recommend *Women's Hockey* to all who wish to play the game and to improve the standard of their own performance.

Doris Crisp
President : A.E.W.H.A.

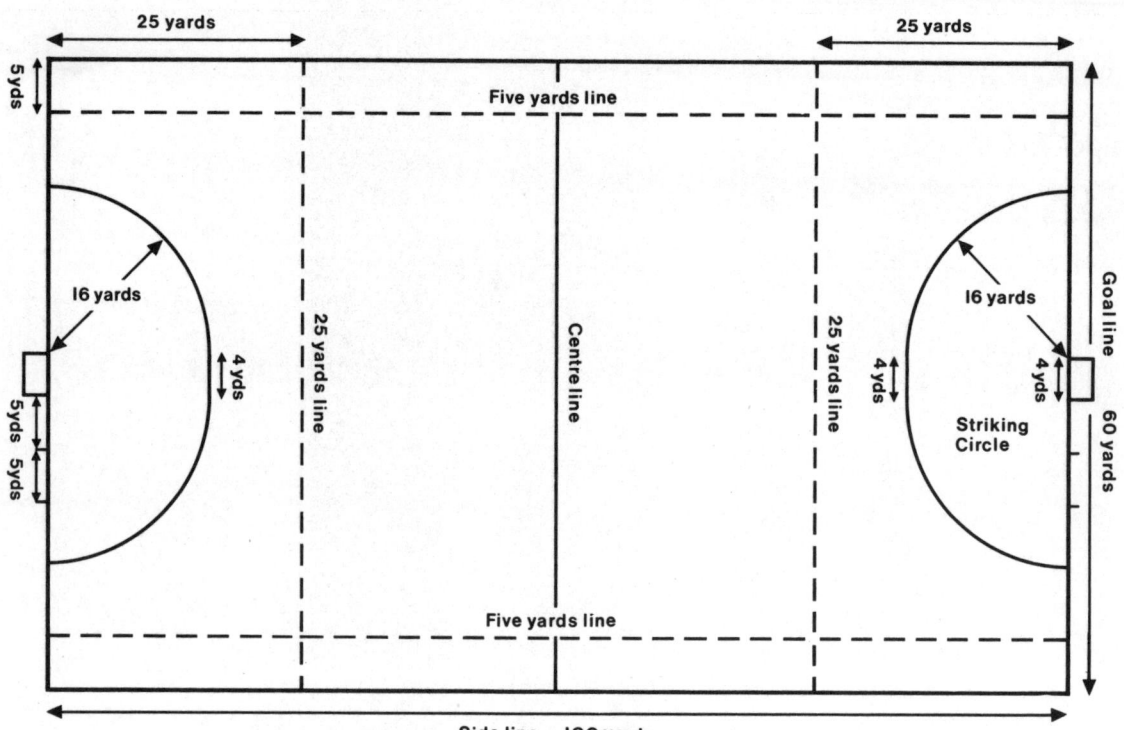

Plan of a hockey pitch

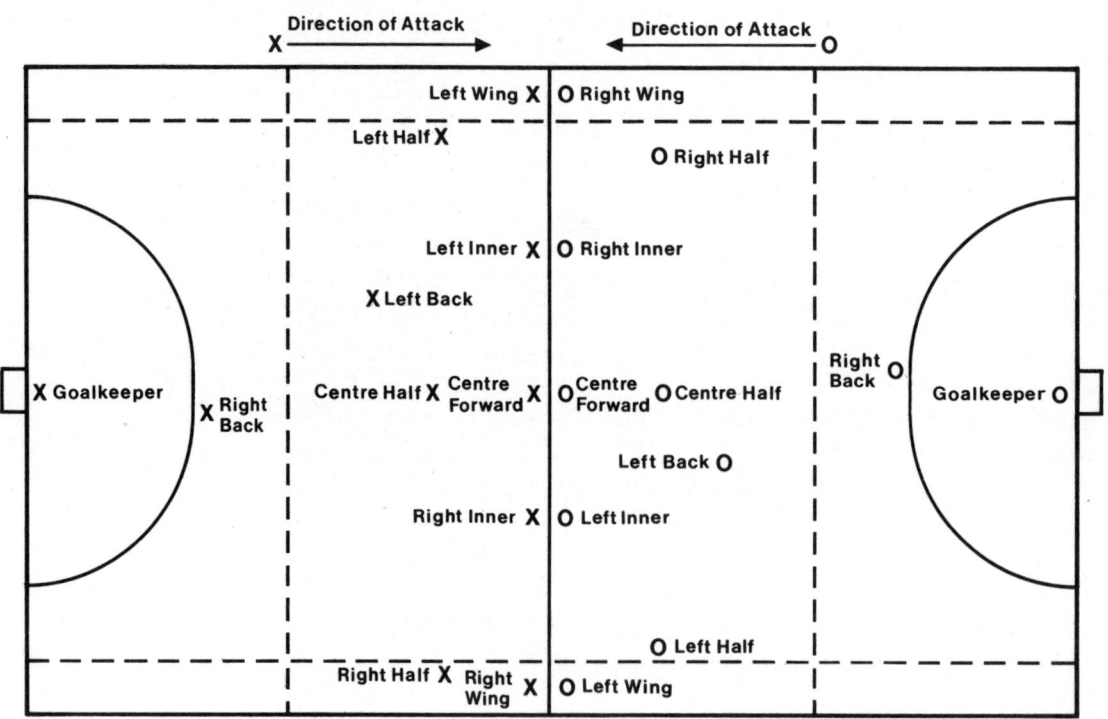

Orthodox position of players

4

Introduction

To be a skilful and successful hockey player you need control of yourself, your stick and the ball at speed. Limited skill means you have limited ideas ; skill is needed to carry out ideas effectively. Accuracy is essential in passing, receiving, dodging, shooting and dribbling. In order to achieve accuracy you have to be able to judge the pace of the ball, the pace of movement of your team, and the pace of your opponents' approach or their recovery if you have them breathing down your neck.

Close control is another essential – a ball running wild from the stick is a ball lost to the opposition. The ball must remain close to the stick so that it is instantly available for any variety of pass, shot or dodge ; whether it be an orthodox hit, a reverse stick hit, a push, a scoop, a flick, or a dodge to the left or right.

Good footwork is vital and this skill can be best achieved by always practising on the move. Hockey is a game of great movement, and skills should be practised with this in mind. Having been shown and having learnt the basic skills in slow motion, speed of action must then be added to give the hockey player the real 'feel' of the game.

Good footwork makes it much easier for you to do what your brain tells you to do and it gives you far more time in which to do it. Imagine you want to pass to the right – the ball is in close control by your stick and you must then get your feet 'twinkling' in order to pivot your body to make the difficult hit to the right.

Footwork and stickwork must be practised together and on the move to achieve skill and success.

Fitness is of the utmost importance. Without it you cannot be in the right place at the right time. It is no use having superb stickwork and footwork without fitness, otherwise you will never have the breath to carry out your skills having run half the length of the field.

Concentration at all times helps you to read the game. You know where to move early on because you have the ability to see moves developing. Anticipating the tactics both of your team and the opposition allows you to save energy.

Never 'switch off' ; think in advance, even though you or your team may not be in possession of the ball. This will help you with your positioning.

Running constructively off the ball into the right space helps your team and hinders the opposition because you create a danger.

Hockey becomes fun if you can outwit your opponents. Often clever thinking can make up for a lack of skill but remember it is impossible to practise your stickwork too much. Even when you feel you have mastered a skill, it needs to be rehearsed and repeatedly practised so that it becomes second nature and you develop into a sharp, reliable player.

CHAPTER ONE

Equipment

The hockey stick should have a thin enough handle for you to be able to manoeuvre it easily. Try gripping the stick and twisting it round with finger and thumb control; if the stick is right for you, this action will feel comfortable. The weight, again, should be suited to you — but the rules state it must not exceed twenty-three ounces. A stick which is too heavy might hit the ball further — but only if you have the strength to lift it! A stick which is too light might be easier to control but it will not provide the weight of shot. Choose your stick for yourself; only you can tell if it 'feels' right. Never have a stick bought for you to 'grow into' — this can be the ruination of your hockey.

The stick must neither be too long nor too short. If the top of the handle is level with your hip bone when the stick is standing upright on the ground, this is the ideal length.

The stick should be bound with adhesive tape if splinters appear, but it must be able to pass through a two-inch ring — in other words, it must not resemble an ancient club!

Hockey boots or shoes with studs should be worn on grass pitches so that you can grip when running and you have less chance of falling if the ground is wet underfoot. The boots or shoes are made of leather or canvas — the leather ones are more expensive but longer lasting. No footwear shall have metal spikes, metal studs or protruding nails. Make sure the footwear fits well. Boots which are too small will make running and quick moving rather painful; boots which are too big will cause blisters.

Wear a thick pair of knee-length socks with a turn-over so that they can be held up by comfortably fitting garters. This keeps a player neat and tidy. Remember, you can always look the part even if your playing ability is not a world beater.

Hockey shorts, divided skirts or wrap-round skirts will be worn according to the school or club uniform. Make sure the button is securely fastened. I have seen a player lose her skirt (and subsequently the ball because she was rather embarrassed!) in an England v. Wales international match (no names to preserve the innocent!).

A cotton or cellular shirt is ideal as it absorbs perspiration yet will not allow you to get chilled. A sweater may be worn to begin with, but do take this off as soon as you are warmed up. Similarly, you should put your sweater on, or drape it round your shoulders, at half time if it is a chilly day, so that you don't start off the second half feeling cold.

Some players like to wear gloves in cold weather but they must be of a thin material – leather or spun cotton – so that the stick can be handled efficiently. Thick woolly gloves or sheepskin mitts might keep your hands warm but you will have a great deal of trouble gripping the stick properly.

I have seen a schoolgirl in the USA wearing a gum shield for protection but I really feel that if you are so nervous and tentative, you should not be playing the sport.

Make sure your hair does not fall into your eyes while playing – this is bound to hamper vision and may make you lose sight of the ball. Clip hair back, fasten it securely into bunches, or wear a head band.

Shin pads are advisable if you have a habit of getting bruised shins. The best type to wear are those which slip neatly down inside the socks. They may be secured with a piece of adhesive tape, but do not have this so tight that it stops your circulation and you finish up with blue legs !

CHAPTER TWO

The Grip and Footwork

The stick should be gripped firmly with the left hand at the top and the right hand beneath it, with the fingers wrapped round as though gripping an axe. The 'old school' used to teach 'together for hitting and apart for dribbling' but as you become more skilled and take part in a higher grade of hockey, it could be more advantageous to keep the hands just six to nine inches apart so that hitting and dribbling take place with the same grip. This 'hands apart' hitting is a skill which is useful when there is little time to slide the hands together – such as after receiving the ball from a corner and shooting at goal.

Never point the forefinger down the handle – this is likely to lead to unnecessary injury.

When running about the field off-the-ball and not involved in any action, just keep the left hand at the top of the handle, but when action is imminent get both hands on the stick, slightly apart, ready for receiving or tackling.

Footwork

Good footwork gives you the ability to swerve, stop, turn quickly, avoid obstruction, and to be in the right position to produce the necessary skill.

The Grip for dribbling; hands apart, fingers wrapped round the stick which is gripped firmly.

Try to remain balanced and never commit yourself with a large step unless you are sure you can win the ball. Try to run on the toes – never be flat-footed even if you feel that way ! Practise quick sidesteps to the left and right to help you with dodging. Often a quick movement of the feet to the right or left while dribbling can get your opponent moving in the wrong direction. A change of pace in your running can set a problem so do not always rush at top speed while dribbling – occasionally slow down, then sharply accelerate, and this can often be as effective as a dodge.

Whether you are a defender or an attacker, you need to have quick acceleration – with or without the ball.

Develop the ability to keep the feet clear of the stick while receiving the ball, but at the same time preparing to be in the right position either to move off in the required direction or to redistribute the ball with the type of stroke necessary for the occasion. For example, as soon as the ball has contacted the stick, get those feet moving ready for your dribble or redistribution of the ball.

CHAPTER THREE

Dribbling

Hands should not be too far apart – six to nine inches – and the ball should be kept very close to the stick with a series of small tapping movements. The ball should be kept slightly outside the right foot and the eyes should be looking down at the ball. An occasional quick glance up will give you the picture of what is happening around and help you to plan your next move.

If you are on the left of the pitch, dribble with the ball slightly behind you on the right to enable a pass to the right to be made more easily. Similarly, if you are on the right of the field, keep the ball ahead of the foot to help with a speedy pass to the left.

As mentioned for footwork (see page 9), change your pace while dribbling as this can be a prelude to dodging. A change of direction (providing your team-mates know how to react) is a useful tactic.

Use your dribbling to cover as much ground as possible, or as much as is necessary for the build-up to your next action.

A slow dribble (providing no one is about to tackle) gives you a chance to look for the player or the space where the ball must be hit.

Dribbling (i). Basic: with hands apart and head over the ball, push it along with a series of small taps, keeping it in control and close to the stick.

A quick dribble can accelerate you away from danger and avoid a tackle that is about to be made.

Also try dribbling very quickly, then stopping dead with the ball trapped by your stick. This will often wrong-foot an opponent or lead her to run past you if she is chasing behind at full pelt.

10

Dribbling (ii). On the left : here the ball is on the player's left ready for a quick hit to the left if necessary. Note how the head is over the stick and the ball, keeping it well in vision.

Dribbling (iii). On the right : keep the ball on the right of the body so that if you want to hit to your right this can be done quickly as the ball is on the correct side of the body.

The Reverse Stick Dribble

This is an advanced skill which should only be tried when you fully understand the obstruction law and know that you must not place your body between your opponent and the ball. If you get into the wrong position, you will place your body between the ball and your opponent and so obstruct.

Keep the ball in front and slightly to the left and it can then be tapped across in front of you as a dodge to the right. The direction of the dribble is across the field and it provides an angle so that the ball can be drawn across the facing opponents and passed straight ahead on their non-stick side.

Reverse stick dribble. The same principle applies — head over the ball and stick close to ball. The toe of the stick turns (left) in to the body and the ball is tapped across the body with (right) the weight transferring from left to right.

CHAPTER FOUR

Dodging

The use of a skilful dodge enables you to meet an opponent and take the ball past them while still maintaining close control. This is not only important in midfield, but particularly in and around the circle where space is restricted. A good player needs to be able to dodge an opponent in several different ways so that they can never anticipate which move you will make.

Five basic moves can be made with the ball to beat an opponent : it can be (1) pulled to the left, round your opponent ; (2) pulled to the right with reverse stick ; (3) pushed round on the right with you running past on the opposite side ; (4) scooped over her stick ; (5) tapped between her feet.

If you are moving towards an opponent your feet must move into the right position before you can start the dodge, otherwise you will get tangled up with the stick and ball.

In the *left pull* (1), keep your feet moving to the left of the ball and move in two right angles with a series of quick taps on the ball : (*a*) forward ; (*b*) left ; (*c*) forward.

In a *pull to the right with reverse stick* (2), the ball has to travel a long way from your left across your body in a sweeping movement, so that it will be out on your right ready to be hit past your opponent on their non-stick side.

The *pushed right dodge* (3) is carried out by placing the ball past your opponent on her non-stick side while you pass her on her stick side and collect the ball on the far side. Be sure the ball is only tapped a *short distance* and *straight* so that you have only a short distance to run before collecting it. Tapping it too far will make you lose control and the ball can then be captured by your opponent.

The scoop over stick (4) is a difficult dodge to disguise, particularly if the ball is moving, because it needs slightly more preparation. The ball is scooped over your opponent's stick with a shovelling motion. The knees must be bent so that you really get down to the ball, and the hips must be lowered. The ball should be well ahead otherwise it is not possible to get the stick under the ball. Keep the hands well apart. (See 'Scoop' page 29.)

The tap between your opponent's feet (5) is a self-explanatory dodge. There is no way in which your opponent can extricate herself quickly to try and tackle back if she wants to avoid obstruction.

Dodges (i). Pull to left. Approach opponent straight (left), then with a sharp movement of the feet, body, stick and ball to your left, swerve past opponent (above right).

Dodges (ii). The reverse stick dribble can be adapted as a dodge by drawing the ball across the face of your opponent and then making a pass to your right or straight – or even dribbling off straight. Note again how the ball is kept close to the body and the head is over the ball.

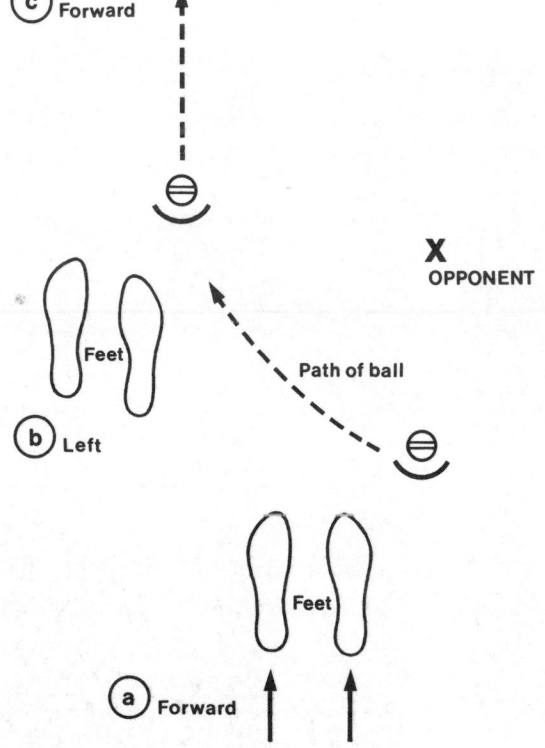

Above : *Left-hand dodge*

Dodges (iii). Non-stick side. As you approach the player, get the ball on your right-hand side (above). *Just as the tackle is about to be made* (below left) *push the ball past on their non-stick side* (below right). *Run round on their stick side and collect the ball behind them.*

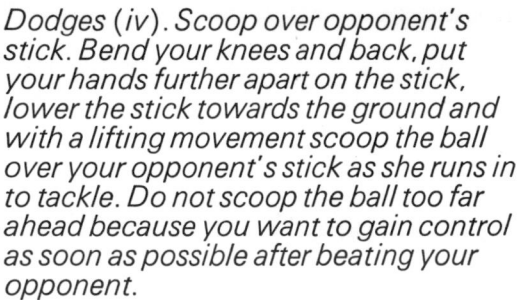

Dodges (iv). Scoop over opponent's stick. Bend your knees and back, put your hands further apart on the stick, lower the stick towards the ground and with a lifting movement scoop the ball over your opponent's stick as she runs in to tackle. Do not scoop the ball too far ahead because you want to gain control as soon as possible after beating your opponent.

If you are on the defensive, with the ball on your stick – not yet on the move and wishing to evade a tackle from an onrushing opponent – any one of the five dodges previously described can be used.

Keep calm when an opponent rushes in to tackle ; plan in advance which dodge you will use and then act quickly. Follow up your dodge by quickly getting the ball under control ready for your next move.

The use of a dodge is much more refined than slamming the ball against your opponent's stick or legs !

Dodges (v). Tapping the ball between opponent's legs. Good timing is needed for this because the movement of pushing the ball between your opponent's legs is left to the last minute – but the dodge is great fun if it succeeds !

15

CHAPTER FIVE

The Bully

The bully starts a game on the centre line, is used if two players commit a foul simultaneously, and restarts a game after injury. All players must stand within their own defending half of the field or nearer their defending goal than the bully when it is being taken.

The feet should be comfortably apart, with the weight on the balls of the feet.

You must stand squarely with your goal-line to your right; do not be afraid to bend your back and keep your head over the ball. The stick on the ground should be close to the ball and the hands should be comfortably apart and gripping strongly. The ground is struck, and then you strike your opponent's stick over the ball *three times alternately*.

The Bully. Ready for the whistle to blow: hands apart, feet squarely astride the line, back bent and head over the ball, weight forward, concentrating on winning the bully.

Try to set the pace of the bully; do not try and imitate your opponent. For example, the first two hits on the ground and against your opponent's stick should be slow but the third hit must be low and fast to enable you to get to the ball first.

Plan beforehand which of the following four methods you will then use to win the ball. Move your feet as soon as the ball is contacted after the third hit in order to (i) help leverage; (ii) avoid obstruction; (iii) move away with the ball; (iv) pass if you are first on the ball.

Methods of Winning a Bully

(1) Pull the ball towards yourself but at the same time step away with your left foot.

The Bully. Methods of winning (i). Pulling the ball towards you. As soon as the third hit of the stick is made, quickly backpedal, drawing the ball towards you away from your opponent's stick. Your feet must move quickly otherwise you will draw the ball on to your legs.

(2) Reverse stick the ball back to a supporting player — but make sure she is aware of this tactic otherwise you might catch her napping!

(3) Push the ball firmly between your opponent's stick and legs.

(4) If both sticks arrive at the ball at the same time, lever the ball over your opponent's stick or pull it away as in (1). Do not take the stick away from the ball, but act quickly and strongly otherwise the ball will be taken from you.

The Bully. Methods of winning (ii). Reverse stick the ball back to your supporting player, then she can receive the pass while you move forward towards the goal you are attacking.

The Bully. Methods of winning (iii). Push the ball with a quick thrust between your opponent's feet. She cannot turn to get herself out of this situation otherwise she will obstruct. Step into the push to give it more power.

The Bully. Methods of winning (iv). The ball is levered over your opponent's stick. Press the ball hard against her stick with your right hand doing much of the pressing. Then, still pressing hard, lift the ball over her stick. Firm wrists and a strong grip are needed.

CHAPTER SIX

Tackling

Several of the points mentioned in the bully apply to tackling. Two hands must be on the stick whenever possible and the feet must move quickly to add support to the stick which is 'searching' and aiming for the ball. Always approach the ball with the stick on the ground, rather like a vacuum-cleaner (but not held like one !).

As soon as you can, try to pull the ball towards you to gain safe possession. This may involve rapid back-pedalling with the feet – small, nippy steps.

Immediately after gaining possession, act quickly by making a speedy dribble or appropriate pass away from your opponent. If, in an emergency, only one hand is used on the stick, i.e. the left hand, get the right hand on as soon as possible to give more control and strength.

Always keep your eyes on the ball while carrying out the tackle. Only when the ball is under control may you allow a quick glance to help you to plan your next move.

The Straight Tackle

Always line the stick up with your opponent's stick and the ball as you move in to tackle. Tackling is a cat-and-mouse game ; try to commit your opponent to make a false and

Tackling (i). Moving in. Stick on the ground; keep weight low to the ground; focus eyes on the ball; place hands well apart on the stick.

hurried move. This can be achieved by pretending to move in to tackle but then halting suddenly. Often, if you move in slightly to your left, this may encourage your opponent to try to pass you on your right. Jabbing the stick at the ball may encourage your opponent to make a hasty move and lose control, and that is when you take over.

Tackling (ii). The straight tackle (left). There is no great swing at the ball — instead the stick moves in along the ground, grips the ball firmly against the opposition's stick and then levers it away. A strong grip is needed to aid the tackle. A straight jab (right) can be used to contact a ball that is out of your normal reach; left hand only and punch away.

If you are beaten in a straight tackle you have then to recover quickly, so never rush into a tackle like a bullet from a gun ! Turn and chase after your fleeing opponent. Steady yourself as you aim the tackle and you will then have more control and be better able to retaliate should you be beaten.

The Chase Tackle

When chasing after an opponent you must get at least level with her before you attempt any sort of tackle. Ideally, you should try and overtake before manoeuvring round to tackle. Keep the feet moving quickly to enable you to face your opponent if possible. If you can chase round from her stick side there will be less chance of obstructing. If you cannot possibly overtake, but you have managed to get alongside, then in an emergency you can carefully swing the stick round with just the left hand in control.

Tackling (iii). Chase tackles. (a) Stick side, one hand. The stick comes down with a sweeping movement and must play the ball, not the stick. Strong wrists are needed for this technique, but it is a useful tackle if your opponent is out of reach if you keep two hands on the stick and seems to be getting away.

From the non-stick side you must try to face your opponent and pull your right shoulder away and out, which will prevent obstruction.

Try to work in a circular movement when tackling on the non-stick side; with two hands on the stick get right across in front and face her, pulling the ball away at the same time. Again, quick footwork is very important for this tackle.

Tackling (iv). Chase tackles. (b) Stick side, two hands. Chase hard after opponent (left), overtake her and then move in to her stick and the ball along the ground (right). This tackle avoids all possibility of obstructing, so if you have the choice of side when chasing, try and get round on the stick side of your opponent.

The Jab

This is more of an emergency tackle carried out on the non-stick side of your opponent, with only the left hand on your stick. With the flat side uppermost (not that you would dream of using the back!) reach across your opponent with a quick jabbing movement. Move the stick

Tackling (v). (a) Jab, non-stick side. When there is not time to get past an opponent on her non-stick side, a one-handed jab may be used but you must keep well clear of her stick and body to avoid obstruction. The jab here is still in contact with the ball and the opposition has overshot the ball.

Tackling (vi). (b) Non-stick side. As soon as possible, try and get into a position so that you are facing your opponent. You must not run across her path in a manner which impedes her progress, therefore get well past before you move in to tackle; stick on the ground, weight behind the stick.

sharply to the ball, then bring it back quickly if you fail, otherwise you will hinder and obstruct your opponent.

If you persist, your opponent may lose control and over-run the ball, and that is when you take over.

The Reverse Stick Tackle

This is an advanced technique and should only be tried when all other tackles have been mastered.

With one or both hands on the stick, get beyond your opponent, face her, pull the ball across and towards you, and back-pedal. Do not run across in front of your opponent.

Tackling (vii). Reverse stick tackle, one-handed, taken just after the ball has been contacted; in this case, the ball has not been cleared away, so the stick must be withdrawn to prevent obstruction. Notice how the tackle is made with the body well away from the attacker.

22

CHAPTER SEVEN

Receiving the Ball

When receiving the ball from a mis-hit pass, get the stick on the ground and line up the face of the stick with the ball as soon as possible. Ideally, a ball should be collected with as much space around as possible, so if you need to create space, move quickly towards the ball initially.

Receiving the ball (i). Basic action. Initially the stick reaches out for the ball and then 'draws' it in under control down by the foot. Note that the head is over the ball; the bottom hand has relaxed its grip so the stick 'gives' as the ball contacts it — hands well apart.

As the stick contacts the ball, keep your hands apart and let the stick 'give' with the impact of the ball. Imagine the stick is a magnet and the ball is made of metal ; the stick drags the ball on to it, and then cushions the impact.

Having received the ball and got it under control, swerve off quickly to get out of danger. Then decide immediately what to do with it.

When receiving from behind, you *must* keep your feet pointing towards the goal which you are attacking. To turn your back on that goal means that you will obstruct any opponent who comes in to tackle. If the pass is not of the correct length, i.e. right on to your stick, you will have to back-pedal to receive it, again to avoid obstruction.

Always 'show' with your stick on the ground where you want the pass. When the pass is coming from your left, the stick face should be out in front, with the flat side facing the left. Receiving a pass correctly from the right is a little more difficult as the stick has to be placed behind the heel and outside the right foot.

Having received and controlled the ball, you are presented with several attacking possibilities :
(1) Pass immediately, (*a*) trying to switch the direction of play to upset

Receiving the ball (ii). From the left. Run the stick along the ground and reach for the ball; adjust the pace of your running so that the ball arrives in front of you; shorten your steps if necessary but, most important, show where you want the pass and keep your eye on the ball — hands apart on the stick again.

the opposition or (*b*) returning the ball to the hitter.

(2) Hold the ball under control and then pass.

(3) Dribble quickly with the ball, then pass when there is a space and an opening.

(4) Go for goal.

The hands should be slightly apart if you mean to dribble off with the ball. They should be even further apart if you intend to trap and hold the ball.

Keep the feet well away from the ball, otherwise you will get tangled up and be unable to work efficiently.

An advanced technique may allow you to receive the ball from the right or from behind with the stick reversed. In this case the ball may be received in front of the feet.

Reverse stick again may be used if the ball is coming from behind on the right and out to the side.

Receiving the ball (iii). From the right. Note that the feet point in the direction of attack. Only the shoulders, body and stick turn round to receive the pass; this prevents obstructing any opposition who come in to tackle. Keep the hands apart and aim to receive the ball alongside your right ankle.

24

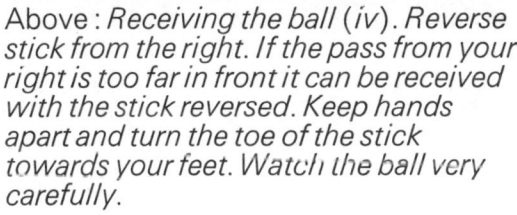

Above : *Receiving the ball (iv). Reverse stick from the right. If the pass from your right is too far in front it can be received with the stick reversed. Keep hands apart and turn the toe of the stick towards your feet. Watch the ball very carefully.*

Above right : *Receiving the ball (v). Reverse stick from behind. A pass which comes from directly behind can be brought under control more quickly if it is received with the stick reversed. Here the stick is about to make contact with the ball 'under the nose' and with a quick adjustment of the feet and a twiddle of the stick you are in a position to dodge, dribble or pass.*

Right : *Receiving the ball (vi). Trapping the ball. A sudden stop from a dribbling run, with the ball trapped by your stick often wrong-foots the opposition. Here the ball is trapped with an angled stick — hands well apart and lean over the ball.*

CHAPTER EIGHT

The Strokes

The Drive

Hands must be together on the stick, gripping tightly, and the wrists and forearm must be firm and strong.

The head must be over the ball, which must be fairly near to the feet.

The left foot steps forward and the stick is swung back smoothly.

The swing of the stick must be fast but not so fast that you snatch at the stroke.

Make the backlift short and away from the ball – not upwards.

Then snap the stick through with power. Follow-through after the ball and make the stick swing through to the

The Strokes (i). The Drive. (Left) Backlift. The head is over ball which is just in front of the left foot after a step has been taken. The stick is swung gently back and away from the ball and then swung through past the body to make contact under the nose. (Right) The hit and follow-through should be firm with hands gripping the stick tightly – and together. Check the stick before it rises above the shoulder, but make the stick point in the direction of the ball.

The Strokes (ii). The Drive-hands apart. A more advanced technique for players with strong wrists. The ball is hit in exactly the same way as in the normal drive except that the back lift is slightly shorter; the hands are slightly apart and the right hand controls the shot rather more than the two hands working together.

The Strokes (iii). Hit to the right. Following a dribble, a hit to the right can be difficult unless you turn at the waist; turn your shoulders and direct your stick through to the right. It will help if you think of pushing your wrists through in that direction as well.

direction in which you want the ball to travel.

After contacting the ball do not collapse the wrists but keep them firm so that the follow-through does not get out of control above the shoulder (which, of course, is a foul).

An advanced technique which might be tried only when the orthodox grip is mastered involves having the hands slightly apart. In this case, the right hand takes over and controls the hit. This is particularly useful for a forward who has received the ball with hands apart at a corner, when there is often not sufficient time to slide the hands together for the hit at goal. Practise this advanced technique in a game-like situation, with the ball being hit out from the back line and a defender rushing towards you trying to gain the ball from you before you can make the shot at goal.

The Strokes (iv). Hit to the left. The ball is contacted under the nose and just in front of the left foot, but instead of swinging the stick face through straight forward, the stick swings across the body from right to left. The backlift, unlike a normal straight drive, tends to swing out to the right rather than straight back.

Women's Hockey

Remember that footwork is important; the feet must be correctly placed for a hit (1) to the left; (2) to the right; (3) straight off the left foot; and (4) straight off the right foot. The pictures on pages 26–27 show this better than describing the action in words.

The Reverse Stick Hit

The reverse stick hit is very useful because it often deceives the opposition. Two more possibilities regarding the direction in which the ball may be hit are offered to the player.

The Strokes (v). Reverse stick hit to the right. (Left) *The swing of the stick is across the body from left to right; the ball is contacted under the nose; the stick must be gripped very firmly and the hands must be slightly apart to give more control.* (Right) *Swing the hips and make the stick follow after the ball keep both arms moving together.*

The grip remains the same as for the drive except that the toe of the stick points in towards the feet. Practise 'twiddling' the stick round from the one grip to the other so that you can suddenly change from being ready for an orthodox hit to being ready for a reverse stick hit. Do not rely on reverse stick play to make up for the fact that you are too lazy to move your feet.

The two extra possibilities are that, without having to alter the position of the feet or the shoulders, the ball may be hit (1) to the right or (2) backwards to a supporting team member without fear of obstructing an approaching opponent.

The Strokes (vi). Reverse stick hit backwards. A very useful decoy if a member of the opposition is coming towards you, about to tackle; a quick turn of the stick and the ball can be hit with a reverse stick to a fellow team member who is following up behind.

The Scoop

A scoop lifts the ball in a controlled manner into a clear space or over an opponent's stick (see page 13).

A shovel grip is used and the stick and hips must be lowered towards the ground so that the stick can get under the ball. The lifting of the ball must involve a movement of the wrists, arms and legs.

Because a scoop is a difficult pass to receive, be sure that it goes into a space so that your team-mate runs on to the ball or the ball runs on to her approach.

The Flick

A flick is a very wristy shot which propels the ball in a controlled manner off the ground, much further than a scoop.

The Strokes (vii). The scoop. The ball is lifted in a controlled manner with a gentle spooning action. It is essential to bend the knees and back; place the stick under the ball and lever upwards with the face of the stick pointing upwards. The right hand plays an important part in this shot by lifting the ball up.

The Strokes (viii). The ready position for the flick or push. The stick has been brought to the ball and the left hand is reaching out in front of the right hand which is well down on the stick. The weight is about to move from the back foot (the right) to the front foot (the left). The level of the follow-through will now determine whether the ball is flicked into the air or pushed along the ground.

Women's Hockey

The stick must be placed to the ball and the hands kept apart ; the left hand reaches out beyond the right hand and then the right hand snaps the stick through and up to waist level, pointing forwards and propelling the ball through the air.

The Strokes (ix). The flick. From the follow-through the stick catapults through, propelling the ball through the air. The right arm has snapped through past the body and helped to lift the ball through the air with great speed. The weight is balanced by the left leg stepping into the shot but the right leg remaining stretched out behind.

The flick is useful because it can lift the ball between two opponents who may be blocking your path and waiting to intercept your pass. It is also a good stroke to use at a free hit – but control it – never direct it up at your opponent's face – and remember it is against the rules to scoop or flick into the circle above the knee level from a free hit.

Try and get the feeling of the stick wrapping round the ball when the flick is being used, and 'throwing' the ball.

The Push

This is a more gentle stroke than the flick and propels the ball along the ground. The action is the same as the flick, with the hands apart and the stick being placed to the ball ; the left hand gets ahead of the right, and then the right hand pushes along after the ball and the stick stays 'glued' to the ball for as long as possible.

The Strokes (x). The push. From the ready position the right hand snaps through but the stick stays very low to the ground, following after the ball. This is where the stroke differs from a flick, in the low follow-through. Note how the arms are really reaching through after the ball and the weight is kept low to the ground. The effort is so great it brings out the double chins!

The ball should be kept out in front and slightly to the right, and the left foot should lead and step into the push. Keep the head over the ball.

To gain more power, the stick may be 'swept' along the ground into the ball.

The push may be used either from a controlled dribble or a free hit. It is not an advisable stroke to use on heavy ground or on a pitch with long grass, if you want the ball to travel any distance. The push is an ideal stroke for a short accurate pass on to the stick as it is easy to receive and control. It is a quickly executed stroke and is useful when under pressure from an imminent tackle. More power can be achieved with greater use of the arms and a greater sweep of the hips.

CHAPTER NINE

Passing

Basically, a pass must have a purpose. The ball can be propelled either into a space or to the stick of a team member. A pass should always be thought out and should never be an aimless forward, sideways or diagonal hit in the hope that one of your team *might* get the ball.

Two people are involved in passing – the giver and the receiver – and each can make it easier for the other by following certain principles.

The receiver should indicate with her stick that she is ready to accept the ball and where she would like it. The giver should answer this availability and make it easy for her partner by making the pass accurately, propelling the ball with the right amount of pace, and timing the pass so that the ball is sent at the right moment.

Develop a wide variety of passes and use any of the strokes previously described, i.e. the drive, scoop, flick, push, or reverse stick drive.

Passing the ball (i). To the right. The body must turn at the waist in order for the ball to be hit to the right. The left foot points in the direction of the hit, as do the hands and the face of the stick. The head must be down and the eyes kept on the ball.

Never 'telegraph' a pass. This is difficult because obviously you have to get your feet and body 'arranged'. Although in your mind you know what type of pass you are going to use, leave the action until the last possible minute.

A pass must be thought out quickly. Decide which is the best type of pass ; whether it has to be made into a space or on to the stick ; how hard the ball must be propelled ; the position of the opposition and whether the ball can avoid their stick and reach.

Nothing is more pointless in the game of hockey than passing the ball without thought. Never make the pass in a certain direction because you *think* one of your team ought to be there. Make sure that she is or will be there before getting into action. Follow the rule of : control, look, think, pass, and you should succeed.

Passing the ball (ii). To the left. The stick swings across the front of the body but the weight is kept balanced by the right leg which stretches out behind. There must be some movement of the hips and shoulders from the right to the left to give the stroke power.

CHAPTER TEN

Shooting

Shoot as soon as the opportunity presents itself unless you are absolutely sure that by manoeuvring you can create a better angle. If you know the goal-keeper's capabilities, you might feel that it is better to move in and place the ball round the goalkeeper.

Never shoot and then relax. Always be prepared to rush in after your shot in case the ball is saved and it rebounds towards you. If you are not the hitter, but another attacker, try and anticipate the shot and move in like a flash on the goalkeeper to pick up any loose clearance.

Try and study the goalkeeper and spot any weakness. If the goalkeeper is good at stopping hard drives, test her with a different type of shot, e.g. a scoop or a flick.

If you are coming in to goal near the back line from a very narrow angle, glance to see if the keeper has left a space between herself and the near post. Feign to pass the ball back and if the goalkeeper moves to anticipate that pass, shoot into the gap she has left.

Make your drive at goal with the minimum of back-lift. This will give less time for the opposition to dispossess the ball from you. Ideally, the drive should aim the ball into the corners of the goal, making it more difficult for the goalkeeper.

Try and use a variety of shots ; never become known for one particular shot. This makes life easy for the goalkeeper.

A flick is an awkward shot for the goalkeeper to save, for the ball is lifted and it will almost certainly spin when it lands on the ground. The flick at knee height is a telling shot and it can be used from the front of the goal or if approaching from the side. Because no back-lift is needed for the flick, this is a good shot to use when you have little time to spare.

An advanced technique can be added to the scoop, which enables you to put a spin on the ball. Flick the ball as described on page 29, but when you have 'thrown' it, roll the blade of the stick over the top of the ball at the last minute.

A scoop can be very useful when shooting, particularly if you notice that the goalkeeper has come off the goal-line too far. A good high scoop might enable you to lift the ball in a safe, controlled way over the goalkeeper's head.

It is very difficult for a goalkeeper to clear the ball first time from a scoop without leading to dangerous play. Therefore, a scoop is a most useful stroke to use, for while the goalkeeper is trying to get the ball under control, forwards can rush in and force the ball into the net.

Shooting at Goal (i). Drive at goal. Shoot as soon as the opportunity presents itself — and aim for the corners of the goal. The goalkeeper has moved out of goal slightly to narrow the angle, so cutting down the amount of space into which the ball can be placed.

Shooting at goal (ii). A flick inside the far post. The attacker has cut into the circle from the left and before the goalkeeper tackles, the ball is flicked, aiming towards the inside of the far post.

CHAPTER ELEVEN

Free Hits and the Sixteen-yard Hit-out

Free hits, in general, should be taken quickly while the opposition still have not repositioned themselves to mark either a player or a space.

There are occasions when it is not possible to take the free hit quickly ; for example, when members of your team are not positioned correctly to receive the hit, or are not ready to run on to the ball which is hit into a space.

If you are not going to gain any tactical advantage by taking the hit quickly, it is far better to pause and look around, and wait for one of your side to make a move, rather than lose possession. Timing is very important both for the hitter and the receiver. The hitter should look around when preparing for the hit, and this preparation should start as soon as you know the free hit is yours. A glance round in all directions should present you with a picture of all the possibilities for your free hit.

Do not advertise where you will hit the ball.

Far better to pretend you are hitting in one direction to get the opposition moving the wrong way – then quickly move your feet and make the hit in another direction.

If you are a defender and gain a free hit in the circle, do not always carry the ball to the edge of the circle for the hit. You can often gain an advantage by taking the hit from the spot where the incident happened – provided, of course, the opposition are safely out of range five yards away !

Receiving a Free Hit

If you want to receive the free hit, you have got to make yourself available. It is no use standing still and hoping that the ball will find its way by magic through a crowd of opposition. You must pull yourself away from the free hit initially, so creating space, and then when you feel your 'hitter' is ready, make a quick darting movement into that space, showing with your stick where you wish to receive the ball, i.e. on your right or left.

Ideally, several of the team receiving the hit should make a move so that the hitter has more than one choice of direction. Only careful timing will make this movement helpful to the hitter. If you move too soon before the hitter is ready, the opposition will spot your move and mark you again.

It is a useful ploy to show complete

disinterest in the free hit initially, so lulling your opponents into thinking that you are not creating a danger. When they are off-guard, that is when you make your quick move.

The Sixteen-yard Hit-out

The same general points apply to the hit-out as to the free hit. The hit is taken level with the outside edge of the circle and in a straight line with the point at which the ball crossed the back line.

The goalkeeper should retrieve the ball very quickly from behind the line while the defender is positioning herself to take the hit. A quick lob from the goalkeeper will get the ball to the hitter, who should be able to relieve the pressure by taking the hit-out quickly and accurately.

It is not always possible for a defender to clear the ball in a forward direction if the opposition are blocking all possibilities. Therefore, one player at least must place herself (at least five yards away) alongside her team member to be in a position to receive a sideways (or square) pass, to get play moving and to draw the opposition away from the available forward-looking spaces.

The ball must be positioned correctly to abide by the rules, but if the pitch has a poor, uneven surface, try to avoid placing the ball in a hollow, which will make it very difficult to hit cleanly.

In your defending twenty-five-yard area of the field, it is usually dangerous to make a cross-field pass for if you hit inaccurately the opposition can pick up the mis-hit, quickly enter the circle and set up a scoring chance.

For a midfield free hit, a cross-field pass opens up the play and often puts the opposition defence on the wrong foot, but again accuracy is most important.

A free hit outside the goal circle which you are attacking is difficult, for the opposition is sure to crowd the area to try to block out any through passes into the circle. Often a pass out to the wings will draw the opposition out of the circle and then the shot or pass into goal can be made more easily.

Make free hits count. Take pride in getting the hit accurately to your team. On occasions, a good free hit from defence can set up an attack which leads to your side scoring — and that makes you feel very important!

Free hits. 16-yard hit-out. The hitter is on the same side as the two players with bibs, but cannot hit-out straight forward because the path is blocked (by two players who were five yards away when the hit was taken but moved in to try and intercept after the hit). Two of the defending team place themselves available for the hit-out, so that the ball can be sent to the nearest defender who then passes the ball to the player on the wing, and so clears the danger.

37

CHAPTER TWELVE

The Roll-in or Push-in

When the ball goes out of play over the side line, a roll-in or push-in is taken by the side who did not put the ball out of play.

In the past, men's and women's hockey always used a roll-in by hand to restart play; men's hockey then adopted a push-in and in 1974 women's hockey throughout the world changed from a roll-in to a push-in.

For the push-in the ball is placed on the line but the taker may step over the line.

For a roll-in the taker must have feet and stick behind the side line. All other players must be five yards away for the push-in or, in the case of a roll-in, must retire behind the five-yard line (women's hockey) or seven-yard line (men's hockey).

Once the roll-in or push-in has been taken, the taker must not play the ball until it has been touched by another player.

The 'roller' or 'pusher' can be helped greatly by the positioning of other team members, who must make themselves available to receive the ball. They must not take up their places and stand still for they can be marked too easily by the opposition.

As in a free hit, the receiver must be prepared to move into a space to shake off any opposition. At a push-in, a player may position herself outside the side line, providing she is five yards away from the ball. If a push-in is taken in an attacking situation, usually the wing and one other player (an inner, or midfield player if the team is playing an unorthodox system) make themselves available for the roll or push.

In a defensive situation the full back nearest to the side line should also be prepared to receive the ball.

If the opposition are taking the roll or push, try to mark closely any opponents who are attempting to receive the ball.

The Roll-in Technique

The roller must bend the knees and make the hand brush the ground as the ball is released; also practise sending the ball out of the back of the hand for deception, so that it can be rolled square or even backwards. This adds a greater variety to the roll and prevents the opposition anticipating your plan.

The push-in (i) *(above) and the roll-in*
(ii) (right). The ball must be placed on
the line and all players must be five yards
away but need not be on the pitch (note
position of wing player). All sticks should
be on the ground. 'Bibs' are ready to
receive and 'non-bibs' are prepared to
intercept.

Until 1974 women's hockey used a
roll-in to start play when the ball passed
over the side-line. In case this technique
returns to the rules, this is how it should
be taken — knees well bent, feet and
stick behind the line, roll the ball along
the ground — do not drop it from a
height!

The Push-in Technique

The push-in employs the same sort of
stroke as a push (see page 30). The ball
is placed on the line. The ball must stay
on the ground and the takers must
develop a hard, flat stroke. If the wrists
are used too much, the push will turn
into a flick, especially if the head is not
over the ball.

As soon as it is known that your team
have gained a push-in, the taker must get
into position quickly so that the
opposition cannot form a ring around the
ball. Receivers must be prepared to move
to the ball once it has been pushed. and
the taker must develop great accuracy to
propel the ball on to a stick or into a space

39

Women's Hockey

where she knows one of her team will arrive to receive the push.

In defence, the defenders must get round the ball with sticks on the ground. Eyes must be glued on that ball and weight must be on the balls of the feet so that a quick move can be made to intercept the push.

In women's hockey, defenders should try to ring the ball five yards away, for rarely is the strength of a woman's wrists sufficient to propel the ball quickly enough to avoid interception.

Roll-in and Push-in Tactics

In both the roll-in and push-in, similar tactics can be used to assist the taker — who should, of course, develop a variety of angles, strength and length to the pass.

In the defending half of the field, a long roll or push just inside the side line will gain a lot of ground and relieve the pressure on the defence. Alternatively, a very short roll or push — just sufficient to get the ball into play over the side line — can be received if an attacker is prepared to make a quick dart to the ball. This quick movement should catch the defence unprepared and allow the attacker to get free.

The attackers who move into position to help the taker can either place themselves in positions to receive the ball or they can move apart and away from the taker, so creating a space for the ball to be rolled or pushed into midfield.

Roll-ins and push-ins are an important part of the game. The technique must be practised to acquire skilful passing of the ball, and tactics must be rehearsed by the takers and the rest of the team. A series of signals can be worked out so that the receivers know which type of pass the taker is going to use — either long or short or with the ball going downfield, midfield, or even back to a waiting team member.

CHAPTER THIRTEEN

Moving Off the Ball

A player in possession is greatly helped if her team members move intelligently 'off the ball'. In other words, even though you are not directly involved in the play, by moving in certain directions you can make it easier for whoever has possession of the ball.

Moving off the ball can help in several different ways; you can act as a decoy by making an opponent mark and follow you, even though you have no intention of receiving a pass. Drawing opponents away creates much more space. This space can be used (i) for the player in

Moving off the ball. The player in the bib needs space to pass out to her right. She will not pass straight because I have moved off the ball taking one of the opposition with me — thus creating space on the right. A reverse stick pull by the player in possession puts the ball on to her right ready for the alternative pass to be made.

Women's Hockey

possession to move through, or (ii) for a pass so that another attacker can 'cut' quickly into the gap to receive the ball. This space is also useful for you to move into to help a player who is under pressure. If two team-members close in on one another, they can be marked by one member of the opposition, but if you keep well spaced out it occupies all of the opposition.

When children first start to play hockey, the great temptation is to run towards the ball in the hope of being able to join in. All this does, however, is to create a crowd of players in a confined space. It is much better to keep clear of the player in possession until the pass is made in your direction.

If all players think about where they are running 'off the ball', they can give the player with the ball a choice of passes.

Imagine, for example, a wing player has the ball but cannot pass to the near inside forward because that player is marked. The inside forward can then make a quick move off the ball to a new position straight ahead of the winger. The winger, spotting this intelligent moving 'off the ball', can pass the ball straight ahead into the space where the inside forward will arrive.

Similarly, a defender can be helped to clear constructively if a team member moves into a space clear of any marking opposition.

CHAPTER FOURTEEN

Penalty Stroke

A penalty stroke replaced a penalty bully in women's hockey in 1974.

A penalty stroke is awarded if, in the opinion of the umpire, a member of the defending team fouls in the circle, and in doing so prevents what would have been a certain goal ; or if a defending member persistently fouls.

Any member of the attacking team may be nominated to take the penalty stroke against the goalkeeper. The goalkeeper may not be allowed any change of dress or equipment. The ball is placed seven yards out from the centre of the goal-line and the attacker may only take one step to the ball. Having taken the stroke, the attacker may not approach the ball or the goalkeeper.

The ball can be pushed, scooped or flicked (see pages 29–31) into any part of the goal at any height – but it may not be hit. The stroke needs to be vigorous to put pace on the ball so that the goalkeeper has little time in which to intercept the shot. The stroke needs to be accurate and the direction should be disguised to prevent anticipation. The shot should be aimed inside the goal-posts.

The goalkeeper has to stand on the goal-line and may not move her feet until the ball is touched. The keeper will not be penalised if the ball rebounds off her body.

It will help the goalkeeper if she crouches ready, feet slightly apart with the weight on the balls of the feet. The stick in the goalkeeper's right hand should be held partway down the handle and she should be prepared to use this on the right if the ball is directed out of the reach of her right foot or leg. She may prefer to hold the stick in both hands so that, if a hand stop is used to save the ball, the stick will still be held by the other hand.

The goalkeeper must watch the ball and her opponent's stick and try to anticipate in which direction the penalty shot will be made. If the goalkeeper saves the stroke, the game is then restarted by a free hit taken by the defending side outside the edge of the circle and opposite the centre of the goal.

The odds are that the attacker will score because the keeper has the encumbrance of kickers and pads which will slightly hamper rapid movement. The goalkeeper should not be prepared to be beaten, however, but should adopt a confident attitude and try to outwit the attacker.

When the stroke is being taken, all other players must retire behind the twenty-five-yard line.

Penalty stroke.
(*i*) (top) *Ready to take the stroke, concentrating on the one step only which is allowed and on where to place the ball into goal.*
(*ii*) (centre) *Steady. The step has been taken and the stick is thrusting behind the ball to produce a powerful flick.*
(*iii*) (left) *The goalkeeper is wrong-footed and the ball passes into goal just inside the post. Often a goalkeeper will commit herself to moving in one specific direction although she may not move until the ball is played; if you spot this, lean towards the one side if you can place the ball in the other direction.*

CHAPTER FIFTEEN

Corners

Provided a corner is well rehearsed between the taker and the receiver, it should result in a shot at goal.

Many different tactics are possible for the defenders as well as the attackers, but there are several basics which have to be followed.

Attacking Tactics

The ball must be hit out from the back line hard, smoothly and very accurately to the stick of the receiver on the edge of the circle. The ball can be sent with a hard, firm push, but this is an advanced technique which requires great wrist strength to enable the ball to get to the edge of the circle and the waiting attackers as quickly as it would if it were hit out.

The long corner — awarded when the ball is hit over the back line unintentionally by a member of the defending team — is taken from a point on the back line five yards in from the corner of the field — or it can be placed five yards up the side line to add a variety to tactics used by the attacking side.

The short corner or penalty corner is taken from the back line at a point at least ten yards from the goal-post, on whichever side of the goal the attacking team prefers. The penalty corner is

awarded for either (i) a foul in the circle by a member of the defending team ; (ii) deliberately hitting the ball off the back line by the defending team.

Members of the attacking team, any number but usually four or five, must be outside the circle ready to receive the corner hit. It is best for them to let the ball come to them because this means the defending team, who run out from behind the back line when the hit is taken, have further to go before they can tackle the attacker in possession of the ball.

The receivers should practise stopping the ball dead so that it is immediately under control and ready to be struck into the goal. The rule requires that the ball has to be controlled before it is hit towards goal. A first-time hit at the ball without controlling it could well lead to danger.

Receivers should practise stopping and hitting almost in one movement. Try stopping the ball with the hands almost together on the stick and sliding the hands up the stick as it is taken back a short way before striking the ball. Obviously, the shorter the back-lift, the quicker the ball can be contacted. A long, slow back-lift gives the defence every chance to gain possession and clear the ball out of the circle.

Corners (i). Ready. The attacker is poised ready to hit the ball out to the waiting forwards at the edge of the circle. The defence players (one out of camera range) are poised, feet and sticks behind the line, ready to rush out as soon as the ball is hit.

Corners (ii). Corner hit taken. The ball is hit firmly to the waiting forwards at the edge of the circle. The six defence players (one is partially obscured) rush out to try and dispossess the forwards before they can shoot.

Corners (iii). (Below) Receiving a corner at the edge of the circle. The ball must be controlled before a shot at goal can be made. The ball is being received while the other forwards are ready to rush in to the goal to pick up any rebounds from the shot, should it be saved. Other attacking players back up the forwards outside the circle so that if the ball is missed they can pass it back into the circle.

Once the ball is controlled, the hitter must be prepared to move her feet so that she is in the correct position for striking the ball. The stopping, controlling, hitting and moving of the feet must all take place in the minimum of time. The ball is best directed to the corners of the goal out of reach of the goalkeeper. For the sake of variety, a flick towards goal can be used instead of a hit, and this can often be a very awkward shot for the goalkeeper to save.

Two attacking team members can combine in a very effective tactic on the edge of the circle. When the ball is struck, one player crouches down on the circle edge and stops the ball with her hand and her team mate (who stands poised alongside) can immediately hit the ball to goal. Providing this is well rehearsed it can be a very useful tactic because less time is needed for the ball to be controlled and hit.

The hand-stopper should direct her fingers down to the ground when stopping the ball, and as soon as she has done this she should move away from the ball to allow the hitter more room for the shot at goal.

The hand-stopper should position herself to the right of the hitter so that she does not hinder the shot ; it is probably better if she stops the ball with her left hand so that she does not have to reach across her body.

Corners should be well rehearsed and the ball can be struck to any of the forwards at the edge of the circle. Often a surprise element is introduced if the ball is hit to the forward furthest away from the corner hit on the far side of the circle. Teams should be prepared to vary the angle of the corner hit, but it is a good thing if a sequence has been worked out in advance so that the receiver is not caught by surprise and she knows exactly when she will be used.

Knowing who will receive the corner hit also means that the other attackers on the edge of the circle can prepare themselves to rush in to the goal as the shot is being made. They will then be in a position to fasten on to any rebounds and get an extra chance to score a goal,

Corners (iv). Handstop. A handstop used to receive a corner (left) leaves the ball controlled for a waiting attacker to hit (right).
Note: fingers pointing down to the ground, watching ball carefully and then stepping back out of the way to allow the hit to be made.

should the first shot be saved but not cleared out of danger. The ideal position for the receiver is in front of goal and not too much to one side. If you imagine lines drawn out from each goal-post to the edge of the circle, the best place for the receiver to be is somewhere between where those lines would meet the side of the circle. This will provide them with the best angles for shots at goal. A shot from a narrow angle, i.e. down towards the back line from the edge of the circle, enables a goalkeeper to block more easily any shot at goal, whereas a shot from the top centre of the circle edge demands a big stretch to either post for the keeper.

If one player is a better striker of the ball than the others it is a good idea for her to receive most of the corner hits. The disadvantage of using the same player for hitting is that the opposition can send their swiftest defender out from the back line to that attacker in an effort to prevent the shot being made.

Occasionally a team has a strong hitter who is a defender, but there is nothing to prevent her from coming up to the circle edge to receive the corner hit, providing adjustments are made to replace her temporarily to fill the gap back in the defence. This must be done in case the corner hit is very inaccurate or badly mis-fielded. In this case, the ball passes beyond the attackers around the edge of the circle, through the backing-up midfield players, and can be picked up by the forwards of the defending side who have been forced by the rules to retire beyond the halfway line until the ball is hit.

Defending Tactics at Corners

Six members of the defending team including the goalkeeper are allowed behind the back line for the corner hit. They may not cross over that line until the corner hit is taken. If they persistently do this, (i) at a long corner – a penalty corner may be awarded ; or (ii) at a short corner – a penalty stroke may be given to the opposition. Before the corner hit is taken, the defenders should each position themselves directly in line with one of their opponents on the circle edge so that they run in a direct line to try and dispossess the opposition. If the attackers place four people at the edge of the circle and four defenders rush out to dispossess or mark them, one defender besides the keeper is free. Now this player can either move out in a supporting role to act as a sweeper to clear any stray ball or tackle any unmarked attacker who bursts through, or she can stand inside the goal-post furthest from the side where the corner is being taken and use herself as a last means of defence should the goalkeeper be beaten. If this defender is used in the latter role, the goalkeeper can advance out two or three yards towards the player who has received the ball at the circle edge to narrow the angle of the shot even more.

CHAPTER SIXTEEN

General Tactics

The game of hockey is geared to either scoring goals or preventing goals being scored. Players are given specific tasks in hockey – some are more concerned with attacking than defending and vice versa, but the modern game of hockey demands that all players should be prepared to adapt to the situation at the time.

The orthodox system described as 5–3–2 involves a team having (*a*) five forwards, who are mainly concerned with scoring goals but are prepared to go back to their defending circle to pick up the clearances from their defenders; (*b*) three half backs, who must back up the forwards in attack, must occasionally be prepared to overlap and go into the opposition's circle to shoot. They must also be fleet of foot in order to get back to their defending circle to mark out the opposing forwards, to help clear the ball out to the waiting forwards and set up an attack; (*c*) two full backs, who are very much concerned with marking opponents or a space, defending in their goal circle, clearing constructively to either the halves or the forwards. They must be prepared to advance upfield as far as the opposition's twenty-five-yard line, but only if the full back has the speed to recover and race back to overtake any forwards of the opposition in possession

of the ball; (*d*) one goalkeeper who must think of herself not only as the last line of defence but also as the first means of attack. A constructive clearance by the goalkeeper can often set up an attack. The goalkeeper should be an agile person who can move about quickly despite the encumbrance of pads and kickers which protect the legs and feet, and she must be adept at kicking the ball – the only privileged player in a hockey team allowed to do such a thing as kick the ball!

Nowadays different playing systems are usually described numerically by such terms as 4–2–4 (four forwards or front runners, two midfield players and four defenders). The two midfield players act as a link between defence and front runners and combine with the four front runners to make six in an attack, or conversely combine with the back four defenders to make six defenders. This arrangement of front runners, midfield players and defenders can be arranged numerically to read 2–4–4 or even 4–2–3–1. The '1' in this case acts as a sweeper at the very back of the defence, working across the whole width of the field and dealing with either the loose ball or the free forward.

In the orthodox 5–3–2 system the

centre half has the job of marking the opposing centre forward and controlling the middle of the pitch in front of the attacking goal circle. If the centre forward wanders out to the side, the centre half either has to follow and mark, which leaves the middle of the field unpatrolled, or she has to mark the middle of the field space with the centre forward roaming free and a potential danger.

The 4–2–3–1 system divides the centre half's job into two ; the centre forward drops back and marks the opposing centre forward which leaves the centre half free to work behind the rest of her defence and in front of the goalkeeper. This allows the backs to move further upfield ahead of the halves and they can tackle and dispossess the opposing inside forwards much sooner.

In 5–3–2, the one full back moves only just beyond the halfway line when the ball is on her side of the field and her forwards are attacking ; the other full back drops back to the edge of the defending circle as a cover. If the ball swings to the other side the full backs shuttle up and back respectively.

In 4–2–3–1, when on the attack one of the full backs leaves her forward whom she marks in midfield or defence, and she joins in with the attack ; the wing halves are now defensive rather than attacking (as in 5–3–2) and they cut out the opposing wings. This now means that all the opposing attackers are marked 'man-to-man' much sooner than in 5–3–2.

In 4–2–3–1, the centre half acts as a sweeper, picking up the through passes and any lone forward who burst through. The full backs are now known as links or midfield players and when either join the

attack they must remember that as soon as an attack breaks down they must race back to mark their opposing forward. If she cannot do this, the sweeper assumes her role and the link drops back to sweeper until the danger is cleared.

The key players in 4–2–3–1 are the two links and the sweeper.

Using any of the 'modern' systems makes great demands on the players' fitness but there are several basics which players in attack, midfield and defence need to know and master. These basics should be learnt by all hockey players so that if they find themselves in unaccustomed roles they will know how to react to the situation.

Attack

To form an attack means that a quick break out from defence is needed. Attacking players must make themselves available to receive passes out from the defence and in addition it is often advisable to leave one, two or possibly three players well up the field to get the attack going as soon as possible. Leaving players upfield also sets a problem for the opposition. They cannot commit all their players to attack because someone is needed to keep an eye on any front runners or ball winners who might be lingering near the halfway line.

An attacker in possession of the ball needs help – she can only occasionally go it alone. Help can be provided by (i) creating space through which she can run, (ii) by creating space into which the ball can be passed, (iii) by drawing opposing defence players away from the ball, or (iv) by moving into a space to make it possible to receive a pass from the player in possession.

When attacking, try to use the full width of the field. This in effect spreads out the opposing defence and makes it possible for a player to produce a solo run through space.

It is unwise for front runners – four, five or six – to keep in a straight line. Beginners are always encouraged to move up the field in a line, but it is more advantageous when you have advanced your play to create a forward-moving attack which is not a straight line, so that more variety of passing can be achieved.

The target is the goal, and whenever possible movement should be in that direction. If the way is blocked, passes might have to be placed to the right or left or even back in order to draw an opponent to the ball, and that is the moment when the ball can be thrust forward.

Opposing defence players have to be eliminated. One way of doing this is with a triangular passing movement between two players.

Each member of a hockey team should also be prepared to beat an opponent while still maintaining possession of the ball. Beginners at hockey tend to gain possession and then just hit the ball hopefully in a forward direction without seeming to mind if anyone happens to be standing in the way. A better, more skilful player will learn to control the ball and beat the advancing opposition with the use of a dodge (see page 12), and then will have a great deal more time to assess the next move and either make the necessary pass or possibly execute another dodge.

Triangular pass. The wing player makes a square pass inside just before she is tackled (above) *and then the player in possession draws an opponent towards her before making the next pass through the space to her wing player who has run ahead* (below).

Attackers must be aware of where the attacking goal circle is and shoot at goal as soon as the opportunity presents itself. Too many players try to 'tee' the ball up in the circle so that it is exactly right for striking. This fiddling allows the opposition time to cover back or to dispossess.

Defence

There are two ways of marking in defence. You must either (i) mark the player or (ii) mark the space into which the ball will come.

In the Circle

If you are defending in your own circle you must position yourself between your opponent and the goal – you must be towards the side where her stick will receive the ball and you must be in a position to intercept the ball before she can gain possession.

51

Marking in the circle must be close so that you deny your opponents any time to control or shoot and prevent them from having any space in which they can manoeuvre. Challenge early so that you hurry the opposition into errors, and keep your stick on the ground so that it acts like a vacuum-cleaner sweeping up any stray ball that comes your way.

Marking in the circle. The right and wrong way to mark. The 'bib' defender nearest the ball is marking correctly — between her opponent and the ball, so that she could cut out a pass. The other 'bib' defender has not moved across enough towards the 'ball-side' of her opponent, and had the ball been passed square across the circle she would have been stretched to reach it before her opponent. The goalkeeper has moved out well to narrow the angle of the shot.

The following diagrams show an orthodox defensive marking system.

You may employ a defensive system where you use person-to-person marking, in the circle. If this is the case, the goalkeeper needs to be very mobile, not only in protecting the goal-line but in acting as a sweeper and covering player, prepared to dart out of goal to pounce on the loose ball or an advancing player in possession of the ball.

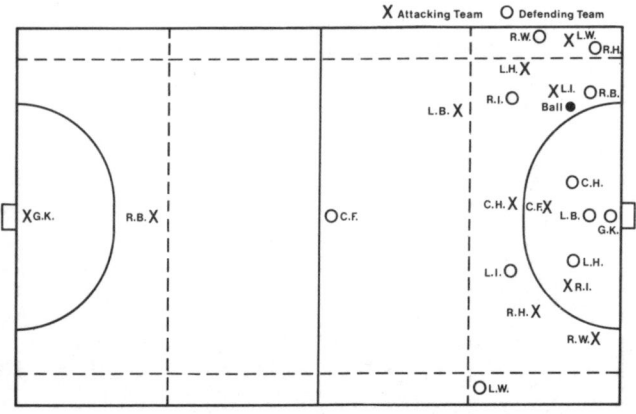

Orthodox defence and attack (left). Note how, in defence, when the ball is on the opposite side of the field, the full back on the other side of the field moves across towards the ball side (L.B.) and her left half (L.H.) moves infield to mark the free inside forward. The attacking right wing is temporarily free but is no danger. Should the ball cross to the right wing, the left back would be advised to discuss with her left half (before the game!) who should make the move out to the wing. (Below left) The 4–2–3–1 system allows the centre forward to drop back; the two full backs progress further upfield; the centre half falls deeper back into defence and acts as a sweeper. The system is more fully described on pages 49–50.

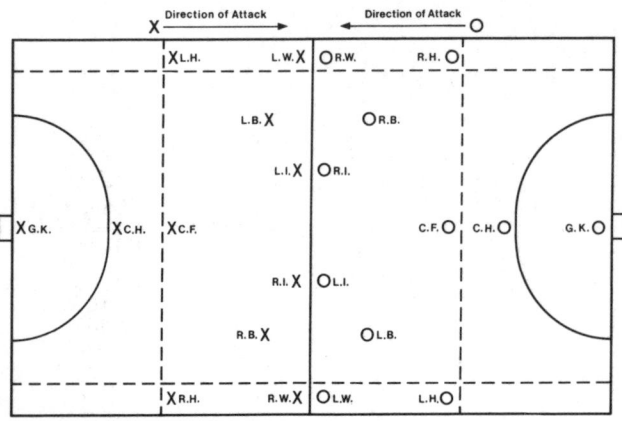

Defending in the Area Between the Twenty-five yard Line and the Halfway Line
In this case you have to mark your

opponent closely, but you stand off two to three yards away so that you are ready to tackle her should she gain possession. Keep this distance between her and the goal and if possible stand facing her or partially turned to the direction from where the ball is coming.

If you gain possession as a defender, it is vital that your clearance is constructive and accurate. Try and have a mental picture of where your team members are so that a quick pass will be picked up by them and an attack will be started. Forwards can assist here by retreating back to their defending circle and making themselves free to pick up a pass out from the circle. This will immediately help to relieve the pressure on a harrassed defence.

In defence, you are constantly turning and twisting one way or another when the opposition moves the ball from one side of the field to the other. This is when you need good, quick footwork so that you can position yourself early to put a tackle into effective use without obstructing.

Midfield Play
A team which dominates the midfield should come out on top. This is where your attacks are successfully built up and where you break down any potential attacks by your opposition.

Midfield players must gain possession of the ball, support their front runners as soon as possible, and be prepared to retreat if the opposition have broken through.

Long passes are particularly effective in midfield : (i) from the left-half position across to the right-wing position (or vice versa) which gets the opposition defence on the move and this pass followed quickly by a through pass will often find them out of position ; (ii) from right- or left-half position or the centre of the field to the corners of the field (or vice versa) is another defence splitting pass ; (iii) from the centre of the field a 'through pass' which travels straight and on the non-stick side of the defending centre midfield player can be picked up by a quick, sprinting centre forward or front runner.

Person-to-person marking is a great asset in midfield, or defence for that matter, so that possession is denied to the other team.

It is a useful tactic to place a triangular defence on the player in possession which prevents the through-ball pass being made.

The use of the defensive triangle in midfield prevents a through pass being made and puts pressure on the player in possession, either to dodge individually or to make a pass square to her right. Her attacker alongside can create more space by moving away, so drawing one of the defence with her (see 'moving off the the ball', page 41).

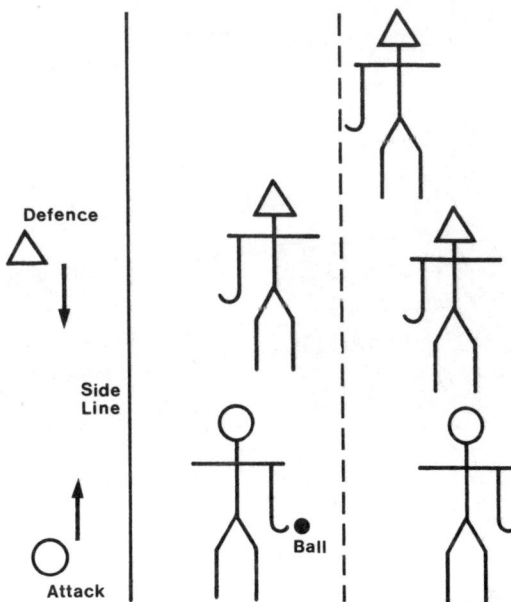

CHAPTER SEVENTEEN

Goalkeeping

A goalkeeper is not only the last line of defence but should also be the first line of attack, for a constructive clearance can lead to the beginnings of an attack.

A goalkeeper must be agile and obviously needs to have the ability to kick with both feet. She should also be properly equipped with neat, well-padded kickers over football boots, well-fitting pads – not too big or too small, gloves to give added protection for a rising shot which may have to be stopped by hand, a warm, comfortably fitting pair of trousers, and one or two sweaters which are sufficient to keep warm but not too bulky so that quick movements are hampered.

The basic kick is made with the inside of the foot and should be a firm, jabbing movement ; the weight – as in all kicks – should be leaning forward and the head should be kept looking downwards over the ball so that it is not kicked dangerously into the air into the path of any on-rushing forwards.

A goalkeeper should always be in the alert position when play comes into her circle ; crouched low so that she can see the ball among the crowd of legs in front of her, weight on the balls of the feet and ready to lunge to the right, left or forwards to dispossess an attacker with the ball.

Goalkeeping (i). Ready for action. A well-equipped goalkeeper neatly padded and with strong kickers; stick held out of the way in right hand so as not to impede kicking; warm protective gloves; loose-fitting jumper (under which several more can be worn on a cold day!); headband to keep hair out of eyes; weight forward ready to move to right or left; concentrating on the game in front.

Goalkeeping (ii). Basic kick (a). Instep. Using the instep, swing the leg through – weight forward, head over the ball, use arms to help balance.

Basic kicks (b). Toe kick. Used to a stationary ball to give more power. A powerful leg swing: the toe is pointed downwards, the head kept over ball and the non-kicking foot must be placed alongside the ball as the kick is made to help your balance.

She should move across the face of the goal following the path of the ball across the circle ; for example, if the ball is down by the back line, the goalkeeper should be right down by the goal-post on that side of the circle. If the focus of play moves to the middle of the circle, she should move out about two yards from the goal-line and in the middle of the goal.

Position by goal-post. This leaves the attacker only one space to aim at – to the goalkeeper's left; hold the post so that you can keep your bearings and push knees together and against the post. The attacker is showing the difficult technique of hitting the ball off the right leg instead of the more orthodox hit off the left leg.

Women's Hockey

If a player is shooting from the edge of the circle, the goalkeeper should move out of goal about three or four yards towards that player, and this will 'narrow the angle'. In other words, cut down the amount of space into which that player can shoot the ball into goal. Having narrowed the angle, the keeper should then be crouched in the alert position waiting for the shot.

Goalkeeping (iv). Ready at a corner. Crouch down, feet and stick behind the line, and look along so that you can see the corner hit being taken, and then you will know instantly which direction the ball is going to take to the edge of the circle.

Goalkeeping (v). Narrowing the angle at a corner. Move out of goal towards the player receiving the ball on the edge of the circle as soon as the corner hit is taken; be poised, weight forward, ready to snap into action when the shot is made. Keep down low so that you can see through any crowd of legs in front of you.

On occasions, an attacker of the opposition will break clear of any defence and move swiftly down the field with only the goalkeeper to beat. When this happens, the goalkeeper must move rapidly out of goal and aim to meet that attacker just as she enters the circle and dispossess her by kicking the ball away.

Goalkeeping (vi). Tackling a lone player. (Above) *Moving out of goal, keeping the weight forward; alert and watching the lone attacker who has broken through the defence on her own.* (Below) *Time your movement to make the tackle just as your opponent enters the circle. Kick the ball away firmly with the instep and keep the body clear to the side of your opponent, thus avoiding a collision.*

A goalkeeper who stays rooted to the goal-line makes herself an 'Aunt Sally' and allows the forward to enter the circle and choose the spot where she wants to shoot.

In general, a goalkeeper should clear the ball with a first-time kick, but if a shot is bouncing awkwardly towards the goal, the keeper would be safer to stop the ball first with both legs together and knees bent, directing the ball down to her feet when she can then kick it clear, or, in an emergency, flick the ball away with her stick. She should not jump at the ball as this will direct it back to the attackers ; it must be kept close to the feet ready for the kick. If the ball is stationary, a toe kick can be used, with the toe pointing straight down, the ankle extended and the leg swinging through and after the ball.

(Below) *Goalkeeping (vii). Stopping a bouncing or lifted shot. Keeping the knees tightly together, bend them downwards at the moment of impact directing the ball to the ground. Do not jump at the ball as this will only cause it to rebound back to the attacker. Head over ball.*

Women's Hockey

If a ball is lifted in a controlled manner at goal, the keeper must avoid the illegal temptation of swinging her stick at the ball. Instead, she may use her hand to stop the ball and direct it perpendicularly down to the ground and then immediately clear the ball out of the circle.

Clearances out of the circle are best sent to the sides. This will clear the danger more than if the ball is put back into a crowd of players. A goalkeeper should have a mental picture of the spaces in front and to the sides so that she can effect the most constructive clearance.

A goalkeeper should always be prepared to lunge to the side or forwards to clear a ball and prevent an attacker getting to it first. If she knows she cannot get to the ball before the attacker, she should then prepare herself and stand in the alert position ready to snap into action and prevent the shot from going into the goal.

A keeper is well padded (or should be !) and therefore should always try and use her feet and legs to kick the ball, but in an emergency she should be prepared to use her stick if the ball is travelling wide and into the goal to her right. The stick should be held in the right hand only and partway down but hanging by the keeper's side, and should only come into use if the feet or legs cannot be used.

Goalkeeping (viii). Handstop followed by toe kick. Get as near to the ball as possible and aim to drop it immediately and perpendicularly (left). As the ball is on its way to the ground, adjust your body so that you can immediately clear to the side with either a toe kick (right) or a kick with the instep.

(Above) *Goalkeeping (ix). Clearing to the side. By turning your body and directing the inside of your kicking foot towards the sideline, it is possible to clear a shot out of danger towards the sides. This clears the ball from the danger area.*

(Below) *Goalkeeping (x). Lunge save. A shot passing wide to one side or the other into goal demands that you produce a lunge save — a good stretch of the legs. Get the inside of the foot to the ball, balance your movement with your arms — but be careful not to wave your stick too high! As your foot contacts the ball you tend to slide across on your heel and this helps direct the ball away from danger.*

Goalkeeping (xi). Stick save. The quickness of the movement of play across a goalmouth often leads to a goalkeeper having to make an emergency stick save. A ball passing wide to the goalkeeper's right can be saved by extending sideways with the stick. Watch the ball very carefully.

Women's Hockey

If a forward is approaching the circle with only the covering full back or sweeper to beat, the keeper should creep out of goal and be ready to tackle that forward if she dodges the covering back, or clear the ball which may run loose as the attacker dodges round the covering back. The back should tackle the forward on the edge of the circle – and should wait for the forward to come to her.

(Above) *Goalkeeping (xii). Working with your defence. One attacker against two defence requires the field player to tackle the opposition just on the edge of the circle. The goalkeeper backs up the action so that if the ball runs loose she is in a position to be able to clear the danger. If the other defender is beaten, she should immediately cover behind the keeper as a last line of defence in case the keeper should be beaten.*

A penalty stroke is awarded to the opposition if, in the umpire's opinion, a goal would probably have been scored but for a breach of the rules in the circle, or if there has been a deliberate foul by the defence within the circle.

The stroke is taken seven yards out from goal and the goalkeeper has the unenviable task of stopping the ball.

60

(See page 43 for the goalkeeper's tactics at a penalty stroke.)

A goalkeeper is an important member of the team and should discuss certain tactics with her other defence members. At a corner, some goalkeepers like one defender to stay in goal, close to one post. This allows the keeper to move slightly further out of goal towards the player receiving the ball on the edge of the circle in order to narrow the angle and block off more of the goal from the shot.

A goalkeeper should talk to the defence around her during the match if it is essential. She should call out if she cannot see – if one of her defence is

(Below) *Goalkeeping (xiii). Penalty stroke. Stand poised on the line, legs well apart for balance, with weight forward ready for a lightning move in either direction. Be prepared to dive and fall to stop the ball with the hand if necessary; some goalkeepers prefer to have their stick held across themselves with both hands so that if a dive and handstop is necessary the other hand retains a grip on the stick, which is required by the rules. Because the goalkeeper is not allowed to move until the ball is struck, it requires acrobatic splits to stop the ball with the foot just inside a post – hence the recommendation to use the hand.*

standing right in line between the attacker with the ball and herself. She should also call 'Mine' if she wants to run and clear a shot, providing she is the best person to make this clearance.

At corners, a keeper should crouch right down behind the goal-line so that she can look along to the attacker taking the hit and thus know exactly which player on the edge of the circle she has to move towards to narrow the angle of the imminent shot.

In general, a goal keeper should avoid giving away corners, but if her defence are disorganised, out of position and under heavy pressure, and she can see no way of clearing the ball with safety, she would be best advised to tap the ball over the back line to relieve the danger.

When a team member is taking a sixteen-yard hit-out, the goalkeeper should be about two yards out of goal towards the player taking that hit, so that if she mis-hits, the keeper is alert and on hand to deal with any shot which may follow as a result of the opposition intercepting the ball.

All goalkeepers need to practise kicking as much as field players need to practise stickwork, and the following Hockey Circuit can be followed by goalkeepers and field players alike – the goalkeeper should, of course, practise with her feet.

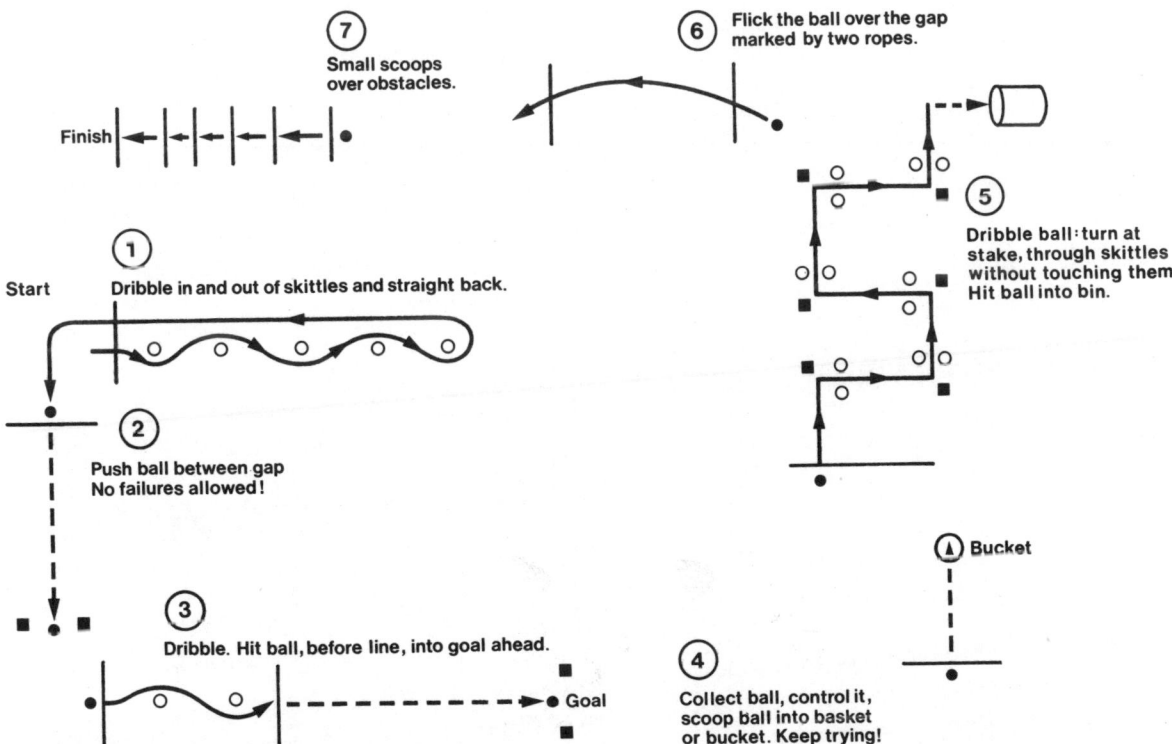

A hockey circuit is an ideal way to practise skills and the use of small apparatus makes the practice more enjoyable and makes the training more of a challenge. The circuit can be used by an individual, or identical circuits can be set up for players to compete against one another. In this case, though, no short-cuts are allowed and each skill must be achieved before progressing on to the next.

CHAPTER EIGHTEEN

The Rules

Teams shall be eleven a side and game shall be played thirty-five minutes each way with five minutes half time. The game shall be controlled by two umpires.

Captains toss for choice of ends and nominate the goalkeeper.

A goal is scored when the ball has passed entirely over the goal-line and under the bar, and must have been hit within the circle or glanced off the stick of a member of the attacking team.

A player is off-side is she is in the same team as the player in possession and if she is nearer her opponent's goal-line than the ball at the moment it is hit or pushed in, unless she is on her own half

The Rules (i) Offside. There must be at least two defending players between an attacker and the goal when the ball is hit. Here you see that one of the 'non-bib' players is offside, for when the ball was hit there was only one player (the goalkeeper) between her and the goal.

of the field or has at least two of her opponents nearer to the goal-line than she is.

There are ten basic fouls which must be avoided. A player shall not:

1 raise any part of her stick above her shoulder when playing or attempting to play the ball;

2 play the ball with the rounded side (the back) of the stick;

3 undercut the ball, hit blindly into an opponent or play the ball in such a way as to cause it to rise dangerously;

4 strike, hit, hook, hold or interfere in any way with her opponent's stick;

5 hit or pass the ball between her own feet;

6 stop the ball on the ground or in the air with any part of the body other than the hand. If a ball is caught it must be released immediately. The foot or leg must not be used to support the stick in order to resist an opponent;

7 pick up, kick, throw or carry the ball in any manner or direction except with the stick.

8 trip, shove, push, charge, strike at or in any way personally handle her opponent;

9 obstruct by running between her opponent and the ball or by interposing herself or her stick as an obstruction. Rough or dangerous play, or, in the case of the goalkeeper, dangerous kicking, shall not be permitted, nor any behaviour which in the umpire's opinion amounts to misconduct;

10 interfere in the game in any way unless her stick is in her hand.

The Rules (ii). Obstruction. How not to tackle from the non-stick side. This is a blatant example of obstruction.

The Rules (iii). Playing the stick and not the ball. A poorly attempted tackle where, although the body is not causing an obstruction, the tackler's stick is not playing the ball but is impeding the stick of the player in possession.

Women's Hockey

At free hits, no player must stand within five yards of the striker, and after taking the hit the striker shall not be allowed to play the ball until it has been touched by another player. The ball must be stationary at a free hit. Any recognised stroke may be used but the ball sent into the circle from a free hit must not rise above knee height.

For rough or dangerous play or misconduct the umpire may :
1 warn the offending player ;
2 suspend her temporarily for not less than five minutes ;
3 suspend her from further participation in the game.

Rough or dangerous play, time-wasting or any behaviour which in the umpire's opinion amounts to misconduct shall not be permitted.

The other rules are dealt with under the various techniques and tactics throughout the book.

Conclusion

Hockey is an enjoyable game and the more skills you acquire, the more you will enjoy playing.

It is a team game for individuals, each of whom should practise all the skills. Much emphasis nowadays is placed on 'systems', 'squads' and 'tactics' but none of these factors will succeed unless each individual team member seeks to become capable of producing all the skills of the game. No 'system' will work unless you can propel the ball with the type of stroke needed for the situation at the time. No 'squads' will become a team without knowledge of all the possible individual skills, and no 'tactics' will work without control and expertise by each player in the team.

Nothing succeeds like hard work, so if you want to succeed in hockey, work hard at acquiring all the skills.

Widen the scope of your hockey by joining an adult club when you are old enough and this may be the stepping-stone to becoming an international player.